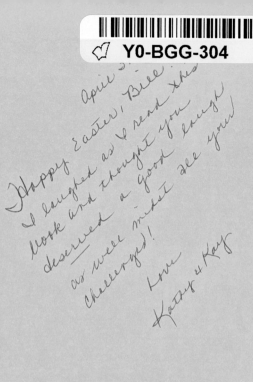

April 3

Happy Easter, Bill —
I laughed as I read this
book and thought you
deserved a good laugh
as well midst all your
challenges!

Love
Kathy & Kay

DON'T CACKLE 'TIL THE EGG IS LAID

Country Proverbs
with Translations for City Folks

Illustrated and Compiled by
T. Bubba Bowdean

Great Quotations Publishing Company

Illustrated and Compiled by
T. Bubba Bowdean

© 1993 Great Quotations, Inc.

Published in the United States by
Great Quotations Publishing Co.
1967 Quincy Court
Glendale Heights, IL 60139

Printed in Hong Kong

ISBN: 1-56245-071-9

INTRODUCTION

Throughout history, every class of people has had their own proverbs, and country folks are no exception.

Truth is, country people probably use more proverb-like expressions in their everyday speech than any other collective group of people. While country proverbs are used in the same way as any other proverbs, the problem is that many non-country folks are often driven almost to drink trying to figure out exactly what the country people are saying.

So, as a service to city folks and to help preserve country proverbs, here's a collection of the best, complete with appropriate translations where necessary.

Never pitch horseshoes
if the horse is still wearing 'em.

Translation:
Never take on a job that's bigger than you are.

Never let the truth stand in the way of a good story.

Translation:
*A good story is worth telling
even if it isn't exactly 100% true.*

The water won't clear up 'til you get the hogs out of the creek.

Translation:
You have to get to the heart of the problem.

Don't wait 'til you're hungry
to go hunting.

Translation:
A hungry hunter won't be patient enough
to shoot straight.

You can't teach a mermaid
to do the splits.

Translation:
Don't spend time trying to do the impossible.

J ust because it thunders
don't mean it's gonna rain.

Translation:
The weather ain't always predictable.

Timing is very important
to the success of a rain dance.

Translation:
Without good timing, your chances for success
are greatly diminished.

You can always tell a Texan,
but you can't tell 'em much.

If you don't make dust, you eat it.

Translation:
If you're not a leader, you're a follower.

A new tune can be played on an old fiddle.

Translation:
Just because something is old doesn't mean it won't work.

Big men leave big tracks.

Translation:
The bigger the person, the bigger the impression.

Just because you give an organ
to the church,
don't mean you get to call
the tunes that are played.

Translation:
Don't be presumptuous.

When you've got it made
in the shade,
be careful that the tree
doesn't fall on you.

Translation:
No matter how good you've got it,
watch out for trouble.

You can take the boy
out of the country,
but you can't take the country
out of the boy.

Translation:
Country roots run all the way to the soul.

Every tub must stand
on its own bottom.

Translation:
Every man has to stand on his own two feet.

Now, don't that just
blow your dress up!

Translation:
Surprises come when you least expect them.

If you start hoeing,
you got to hoe
to the end of the row.

Translation:
If you start a job, finish it.

A good dog is hard to keep
under the porch.

Translation:
It's difficult to hold back a good person.

Flowers that bloom too early
are fair game for an early frost.

Translation:
Being overanxious is sometimes dangerous.

There never has been a horse
that can't be rode
or a cowboy that can't be throw'd.

Translation:
Even the best lose now and then.

If a fox chases two rabbits,
he won't catch either one.

Translation:
Concentrate on doing one thing at a time.

A bird can't fly on one wing.

Translation:
Being half prepared is the same
as not being prepared.

No fish was ever caught with a wish.

Translation:
You have to work at it to be successful.

If you grab a bull's tail, you'll see the horns.

Translation:
If you go looking for trouble,
you'll usually find it.

When you go huntin' remember,
if you hear a "moo,"
it ain't necessarily a moose.

Translation:
Sometimes, things aren't what they seem.

If you don't bite, don't growl.

Translation:
Don't let your mouth overload your capabilities.

No matter how much
you like the hat,
if it blows off into the creek
don't go after it if you can't swim.

Translation:
Sometimes you have to listen to your head,
not your heart.

Don't burn your tongue
in someone else's coffee.

Translation:
Mind your own business.

Sometimes you have to
give a sucker an even break.

Translation:
W. C. Fields said never give a sucker
an even break,
but Fields wasn't a cattleman.

Roosters crow, hens deliver.

Translation:
While a man is talking about it,
a woman is doing it.

Don't make love by the front gate,
'cause love may be blind
but the neighbors ain't.

Translation:
Be discrete.

There is only one good horse
in the country,
and every cowboy thinks it's his.

Translation:
Everyone has his own opinion.

What goes around
comes around.

Translation:
Sooner or later, everybody gets even.

Never let seeds keep you
from enjoying the watermelon.

Translation:
Don't let small distractions
keep you from having a good time.

The best time to buy an umbrella
is in the 4th year
of a 5-year drought.

Translation:
Be a smart shopper.

The hand that rocks the cradle
can also make a fist.

Translation:
Never underestimate a woman.

If you stand under a good tree,
you'll get good shade.

Translation:
Pick your spots wisely.

Love is like lightning;
it's apt to strike an outhouse
as a mansion.

Translation:
Love is blind.

If you have to fight,
make sure you don't have
the short stick.

Translation:
Never let the other fella get the upper hand.

Bad breath is better
than no breath a'tall.

Translation:
Occasionally a bad alternative
is better than no alternative.

Don't kick
before you are spurred.

Translation:
Don't anticipate the worst.

ℒ ℒ

Don't waste your breath
whistling in a graveyard.

Translation:
Ghosts ain't afraid of whistling.

Just because a chicken has wings
don't mean she can fly.

Translation:
Looks can be deceiving.

If you shovel manure
you're gonna get some of it
on your boots.

Translation:
If you talk bad about someone, both of you lose.

A dog that'll hunt
helps fill the dinner table
but one that won't hunt
is just another mouth to feed.

Translation:
You have to work to earn your keep.

If you hitch a mule
with a mountain lion,
the wagon won't get pulled far.

Translation:
If people don't get along well
nothing will get done well.

Even the meanest bull
can be ridden at a cafe.

Translation:
Anyone can "talk" about
the bulls they've ridden
while waiting for the food to cook.

A person's body
is like a bar of soap,
it wears down with repeated use.

Translation:
Be careful about exercising too much.
It could kill you.

You can put earrings on a sow,
but you still wouldn't want
to take her to a dance.

Translation:
You can't turn someone
into something they are not.

Never sign anything
by the glow of a neon light.

Translation:
It's better to be sober when signing anything.

Twenty yards to the outhouse
seems like a mile
on a cold winter morning.

Translation:
Perceived distance varies
according to the circumstances.

If you have a $50 horse
you don't need a $1,500 saddle.

Translation:
Don't waste money on frills.

If you have to shoot, shoot low if they're ridin' Shetlands.

Translation:
You have to make adjustments due to circumstances.

It's better to marry a woman who can cook but won't than to marry a woman who can't cook but does.

Translation:
Eating out a lot is preferable to having to lie to your wife about her cooking.

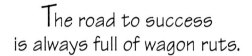

The road to success
is always full of wagon ruts.

Translation:
Nobody said life was going to be easy.

A good scare is worth more
than good advice.

Translation:
Until you have a really close call,
you never really believe warnings.

Be sure you can always
look yourself in the eye.

Translation:
Don't try to fool the face in the mirror.

You got to go
where the buffalo are.

Translation:
You have to go to the opportunity
rather than waiting for the opportunity
to come to you.

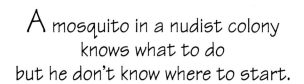

A mosquito in a nudist colony
knows what to do
but he don't know where to start.

Translation:
Just knowing what to do isn't enough.

If you buckle before you swash,
you'll never be a swashbuckler.

Translation:
Avoid peaking too soon.

Company, like corn bread,
goes stale after three days.

Translation:
Don't overstay your welcome.

Don't try to get all the 'possums
up one tree.

Translation:
Diversify.

If there's gonna be three
in the pickup,
always sit in the middle.

Translation:
If you sit in the middle,
you don't have to drive or open any gates.

Breakfast is the most important
meal of the day,
'cause if you ain't home before then
you could be in serious trouble.

Translation:
If you don't get home 'til after breakfast,
you can't swear you slept on the couch.

You always eat better
when company comes calling.

Translation:
Somehow there's always something good
to serve the company.

Don't go around stepping on people
because you may come back
as a cockroach someday.

Translation:
Be nice to people.

The anvil always outlasts
the hammer.

Translation:
The strong survive
no matter how much they are pounded on.

You can't sweep sunshine
off the porch.

Translation:
Don't try the impossible.

If you ain't skinning
you can hold a leg.

Translation:
There's always something you can do.

Never try to teach a pig to sing:
because first, pigs can't sing;
and second,
you'll just make the pig mad.

Translation:
Don't go out of your way looking for trouble.

You can get more pigs in the pen
by throwing corn instead of rocks.

Translation:
You get more cooperation by being cooperative.

You can't tell which way
the train went
by looking at the tracks.

Translation:
Be observant.

The best fertilizer
for a piece of ground
is the footprints of the owner.

Translation:
Owners take care of property
better than renters.

Two kinds of cowboys
ain't worth a damn:
them that never do
what they're told
and them that never do anything
except what they're told.

Translation:
Hire someone who will do what he's told
and go looking for something else to do
when he's finished.

If you give a cow a choice she'll go out the wrong gate.

Translation:
If you want someone to do something, don't give them choices.

A coyote will fool with chickens 'til he feels the buckshot in his behind.

Translation:
If your gonna keep chickens, keep a shotgun as well.

The difference between corn
and cotton is the stoopin'.

Translation:
Some things require a little more effort.

An empty sack
can't stand up by itself.

Translation:
You have to have substance to be independent.

Always know where you're from
'cause you might not always know
where you're going.

Translation:
Never forget your roots or your raising.

He knows everything
there is to know
about cows, sows and plows.

Translation:
He is a very experienced farmer.

A good horse is one
that will stand without hitching.

Translation:
The best person is one that can be trusted
even when not being controlled.

You can be a good loser,
but you should always
bleed a little.

Translation:
If losing doesn't hurt you shouldn't be playing.

If you put all your eggs
in one basket,
keep a good eye on that basket.

Translation:
If you're going to put
all your assets in one place,
make sure it's a safe place.

You gotta dance with who brung ya.

Translation:
Be loyal to the one you are with.

Eat all you can, can what you can't.

Translation:
Don't be wasteful.

You can't raise cattle
by shootin' bull.

Translation:
Talkin' about it don't get the job done.

The time to kill a snake
is when he raises his head.

Translation:
If you don't take care of problems
when they occur,
the problem may take care of you.

If you're low on feed,
feed the horses you ride.

Translation:
Take care of the equipment
that takes care of you.

It's not the size of the dog
in the fight that counts,
it's the size of the fight
in the dog.

Translation:
Size doesn't count as much as determination.

The biggest fish
are usually caught by the tail.

Translation:
Never believe a fisherman
unless you see the fish.

An empty bucket
makes more noise
than a full one when kicked.

Translation:
An intelligent person needs fewer words
to express himself.

Never learn how to iron.

Translation:
Somebody'll always want you to do it.

No matter how warm
the sunshine,
the cat will always
have her kittens in the barn.

Translation:
Old habits are hard to break.

Once you're on the ground
don't worry about the horse
throwing you.

Translation:
The time to worry
is before the horse throws you.

On a mule team,
the scenery is the same
for all the mules
except the leaders.

Translation:
Strive to be a leader
so you always have fresh scenery.

If you play poker with the devil
there ain't no limit.

Translation:
The stakes are high
when you gamble with your soul.

If you cut your own firewood
it will warm you twice.

Translation:
There is more satisfaction
in doing things yourself.

Burnin' daylight
won't keep you warm.

Translation:
If you don't work, you might freeze to death.

Never buy a cow if you can milk one
through the fence.

Translation:
Don't spend money on equipment
if you can get by without it.

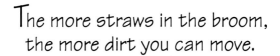

The more straws in the broom,
the more dirt you can move.

Translation:
The better the equipment
the better the performance.

If the horse is already
out of the barn
leave the door open
in case he comes back.

Translation:
Never close the door to opportunity.

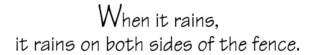

When it rains,
it rains on both sides of the fence.

Translation:
Don't use weather as an excuse.

Just because he's wearin' boots
don't mean he's a cowboy.

Translation:
Clothes don't make the man.

DON'T CACKLE
'TIL THE EGG
IS LAID

ABOUT THE AUTHOR/ARTIST

T. Bubba Bowdean was born "several years ago" in a suburb of Detroit, Texas. He grew up on a sprawling 32 acre "franch" (combination farm and ranch) just north of Cleveland, Texas.

After graduation from the school of hard knocks, Bubba earned a Bachelor of Science in Possumology from The International Possum Institute in Rhonesboro, Texas. He served as possum consultant for the law firm of Oui, Sueum, and Howl until he decided to give politics a whirl.

Following an unsuccessful bid to become mayor of Beverly Hills, Texas, Bubba went back to his roots and joined the pit crew of the Sparks International Armadillo Racing Team. He currently manages a combination veterinary clinic and taxidermy shop which has the motto "One way or another, you get your dog back."